THE PHILLIP KEVEREN SERIES PIANO SOLO

CHRISTMAS STANDARDS

15 ELEGANT ARRANGEMENTS BY PHILLIP KEVEREN

— PIANO LEVEL —
INTERMEDIATE TO EARLY ADVANCED

ISBN 978-1-70519-984-8

Visit Hal Leonard Online at
www.halleonard.com

Visit Phillip at
www.phillipkeveren.com

World headquarters, contact:
Hal Leonard
7777 West Bluemound Road
Milwaukee, WI 53213
Email: info@halleonard.com

In Europe, contact:
Hal Leonard Europe Limited
1 Red Place
London, W1K 6PL
Email: info@halleonardeurope.com

In Australia, contact:
Hal Leonard Australia Pty. Ltd.
4 Lentara Court
Cheltenham, Victoria, 3192 Australia
Email: info@halleonard.com.au

PREFACE

These arrangements were first published in 1994. That Christmas folio is now out of print, but we felt the settings were "evergreen" enough to be presented once again – freshly edited and engraved.

Playing through arrangements penned nearly 30 years ago has been a sentimental experience. I really do not remember writing them, but I sure remember the Christmases from that season of life. Our children were very young. Come to think of it, they were about the same ages as our grandchildren in this current stage of life!

I hope you enjoy playing these magical, timeless Christmas songs at the piano.

Merry Christmas!

Phillip Keveren

July 2023

BIOGRAPHY

Phillip Keveren, a multi-talented keyboard artist and composer, writes original works in a variety of genres from piano solo to symphonic orchestra. He gives frequent concerts and workshops for teachers and their students in the United States, Canada, Europe, and Asia. Mr. Keveren holds a B.M. in composition from California State University Northridge and a M.M. in composition from the University of Southern California.

THE CHRISTMAS SONG
(Chestnuts Roasting on an Open Fire)

Music and Lyric by MEL TORMÉ
and ROBERT WELLS
Arranged by Phillip Keveren

12
15
mf
p
3
18
3
mp
21
24

27
mf
3
broaden
f
30
p
33
To Coda
cresc.
rit.
3
mf
mp
36
D.S. al Coda
CODA
a tempo
39
L.H.
p
rit.
8va
pp

BLUE CHRISTMAS

Words and Music by BILLY HAYES
and JAY JOHNSON
Arranged by Phillip Keveren

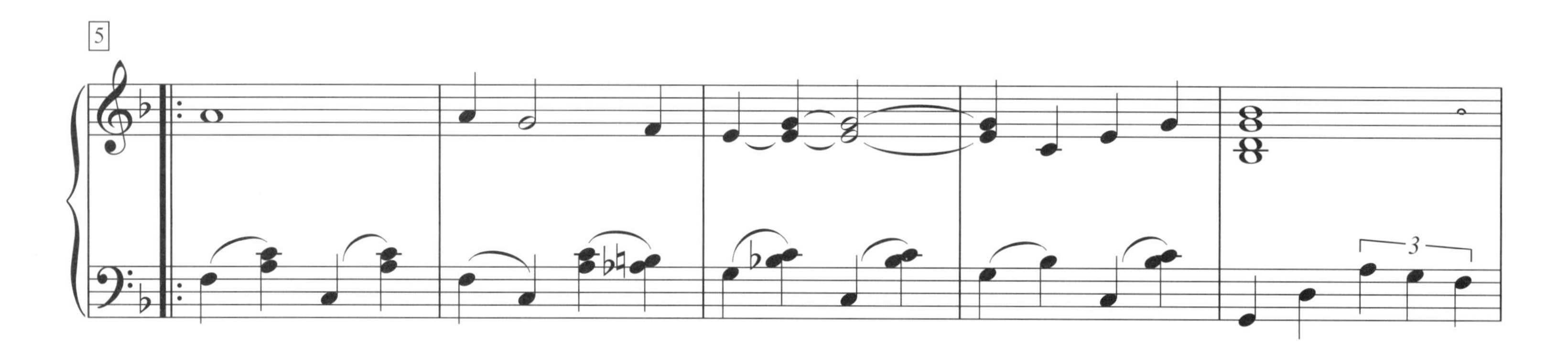

19
poco rit.
a tempo
24
cresc.
29
f
rit. (on repeat)
mp
33
1.
2.
rubato
38
mp

THE CHRISTMAS WALTZ

Words by SAMMY CAHN
Music by JULE STYNE
Arranged by Phillip Keveren

cresc.
f
p
cresc.
f
mf
1.
2.
8va
pp
mp
rit.
mp

FELIZ NAVIDAD

Music and Lyrics by
JOSÉ FELICIANO
Arranged by Phillip Keveren

17
mp
21
mf
24
28
32
f

(There's No Place Like)

HOME FOR THE HOLIDAYS

Words and Music by AL STILLMAN
and ROBERT ALLEN
Arranged by Phillip Keveren

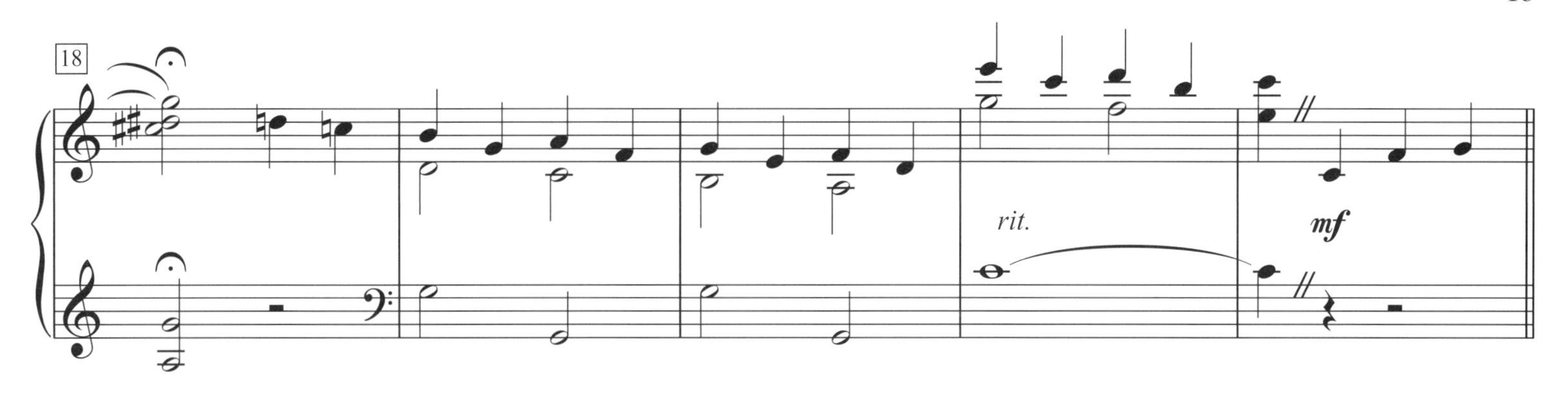
18
rit.
mf

23
Medium bright Country

a tempo

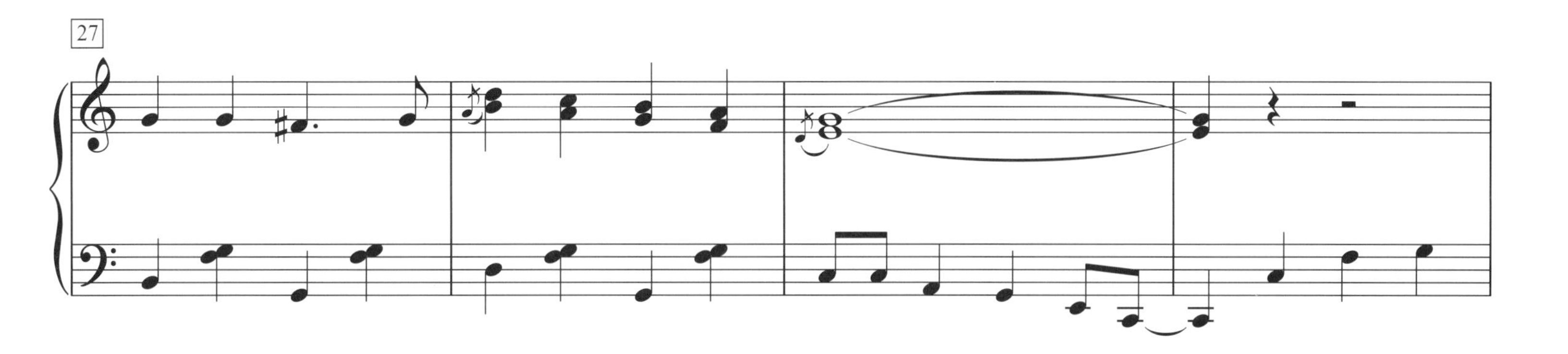
27

31

35
poco rit.

Tempo I
39
43
47
f
mp
51
55
molto rit.
p

SILVER BELLS

from the Paramount Picture THE LEMON DROP KID

Words and Music by JAY LIVINGSTON
and RAY EVANS
Arranged by Phillip Keveren

22
27
32
p
mp
8va
37
mf
42
To Coda

47
mp
52
57
D.S. al Coda
CODA
mf
61
rit.
p a tempo
66
cresc.
rit.
mf
pp

I'LL BE HOME FOR CHRISTMAS

Words and Music by KIM GANNON
and WALTER KENT
Arranged by Phillip Keveren

47
mp
52
57
D.S. al Coda
CODA
mf
61
rit.
p a tempo
66
cresc.
rit.
mf
pp

I'LL BE HOME FOR CHRISTMAS

Words and Music by KIM GANNON
and WALTER KENT
Arranged by Phillip Keveren

21
mf
25
29
f
8va
33
Maestoso
To Coda
dim.
p
37
mp
43
D.S. al Coda
CODA
molto rit.
mf
p

IT'S BEGINNING TO LOOK LIKE CHRISTMAS

By MEREDITH WILLSON
Arranged by Phillip Keveren

15
To Coda
mf
f
3
18
p
21
mf
mp
24
D.S. al Coda
CODA
27
sfz
8vb

LET IT SNOW! LET IT SNOW! LET IT SNOW!

Words and Music by SAMMY CAHN
and JULE STYNE
Arranged by Phillip Keveren

16
p
20
f
mf
24
28
f
mp
32
rit.
sfz
a tempo

LET'S HAVE AN OLD FASHIONED CHRISTMAS

Lyric by LARRY CONLEY
Music by JOE SOLOMON
Arranged by Phillip Keveren

20
mf
25
29
cresc.
f
poco rit.
p
poco accel.
34
f a tempo
mf
molto rit. on repeat
1.
39
mp
2.
freely
p

THE MOST WONDERFUL TIME OF THE YEAR

Words and Music by EDDIE POLA
and GEORGE WYLE
Arranged by Phillip Keveren

17
cresc.
mf
22
mp
26
mf
1.
30
mp
2.
35

40
p sub.
45
cresc.
mf
50
mf
55
60

65
70
f
p cresc.
75
mf
80
f
85
dim.
p
sfz

TENNESSEE CHRISTMAS

Words and Music by AMY GRANT
and GARY CHAPMAN
Arranged by Phillip Keveren

13
mp
16
19
22
25

28

31
mf

34

37
mp
To Coda
1.

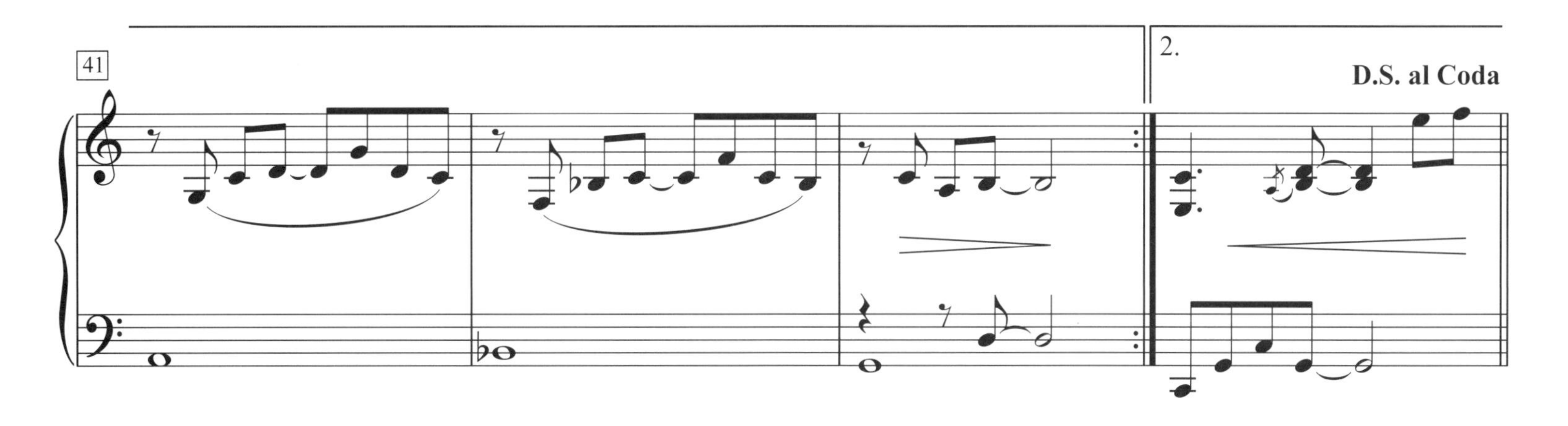
41
2.
D.S. al Coda

CODA

48
rit.
a tempo

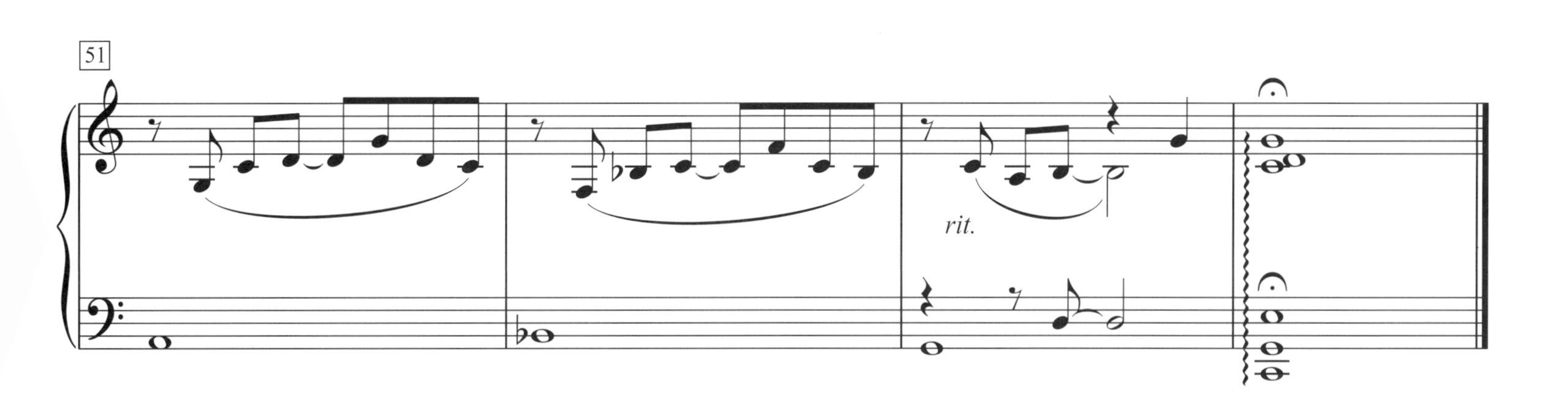
51
rit.

WE NEED A LITTLE CHRISTMAS

from MAME

Music and Lyric by
JERRY HERMAN
Arranged by Philip Keveren

24
mp
f
28
p sub.
33
To Coda
f
37
1.
3
1
41
2.
D.S. al Coda
p sub.
CODA
ff

YOU'RE ALL I WANT FOR CHRISTMAS

Words and Music by GLEN MOORE
and SEGER ELLIS
Arranged by Phillip Keveren

17
8va
mp
22
cresc.
27
f
31
rall.
mf
a tempo
35
1.
2.
mp
molto rit.

WHAT ARE YOU DOING NEW YEAR'S EVE?

By FRANK LOESSER
Arranged by Phillip Keveren

14
17
mf
mp
20
23
p poco a poco cresc.
27
mf

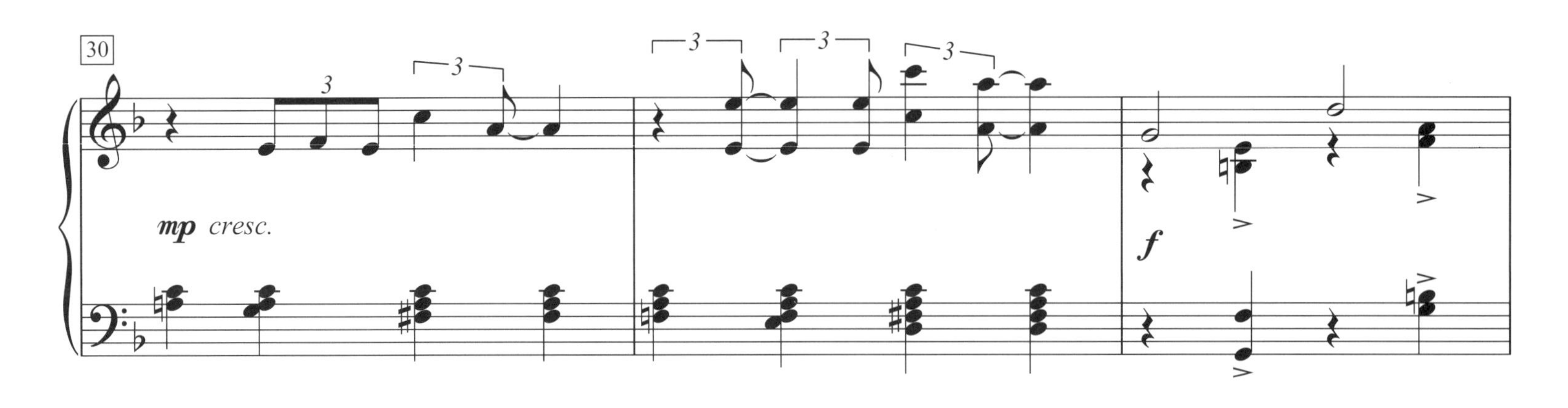
30
mp cresc.
f

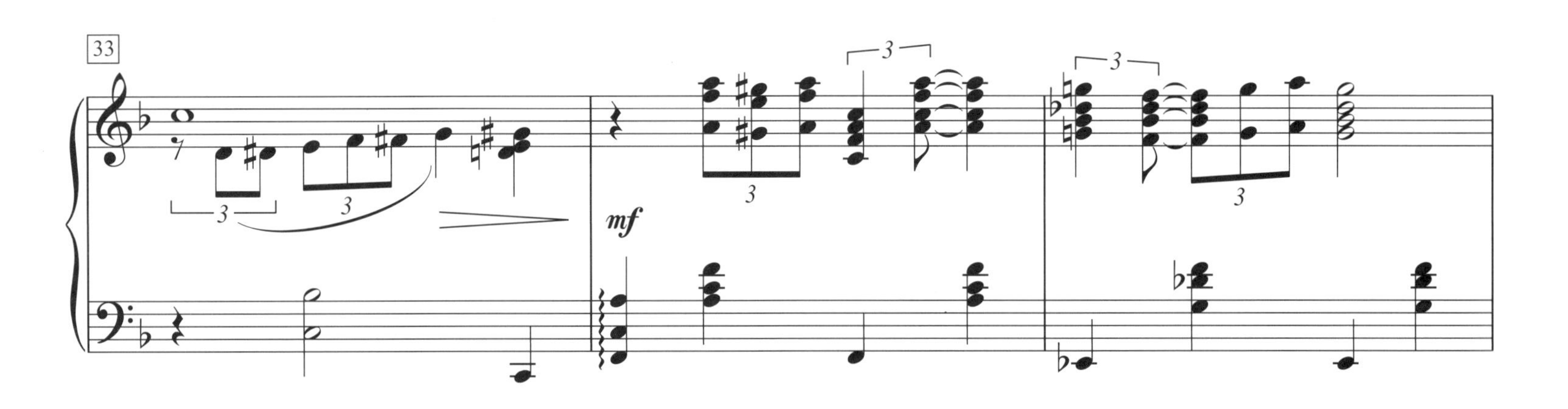
33
mf

36

39
rit. e dim.
p
pp